THE STORY BEHIND THE SONGS

Carmen Mills

CARMEN MILLS

The Story Behind the Songs
Trilogy Christian Publishers
A Wholly Owned Subsidary of Trinity Broadcasting Network
2442 Michelle Drive
Tustin, CA 92780

For information, address Trilogy Christian Publishing
Rights Department, 2442 Michelle Drive, Tustin, Ca 92780.
Trilogy Christian Publishing/ TBN and colophon are trademarks of Trinity Broadcasting Network.
For information about special discounts for bulk purchases, please contact Trilogy Christian Publishing.
Manufactured in the United States of America
Trilogy Disclaimer: The views and content expressed in this book are those of the author and may not necessarily reflect the views and doctrine of Trilogy Christian Publishing or the Trinity Broadcasting Network.
10 9 8 7 6 5 4 3 2 1
Library of Congress Cataloging-in-Publication Data is available.
ISBN: 979-8-88738-521-1
ISBN: 979-8-88738-522-8

Dedications:

This book is dedicated to Milre Lisso, a missionary in Costa Rica who has worked tirelessly to help orphaned children find a home. I know I'm just one of the many whom she has given this gift. Not only did she work in Costa Rica, but she came to the USA to go from church to church pleading with congregations to help support or adopt these children.

This book is also dedicated to Steve and Mary Crane. Thank you for all the hard work of adopting me and all the other children you took in and fostered over the years. I love and appreciate you both deeply.

Especially thank you to Robb Mills. You have been there through all the good and difficult times. When we didn't understand why I was struggling, you never gave up on us. You are one of the biggest blessings in my life.

Melana, Merissa, Michaela, and Miranda, all four of you girls truly are a miracle. I am beyond blessed!

Love, mom

Chapter 1: Reflection

I will give thanks to you, Lord with all my heart; I will tell of all your wonderful deeds. I will be glad and rejoice in you; I will sing the praises of your name, O Most High.

Psalms 9;1-2

I've always believed that the Lord has a purpose and plan for each one's life. After all, why would he take a skinny, malnourished, untrusting child out of her difficult environment and bring her to a well blessed country. When I was an infant, I was taken away from the place I had been living. The woman taking care of me did not provide food and I was starving to death (literally). Where was my mother? I don't know. All I've heard is that she was very poor and gave me to a friend. Since my mom's friend didn't feed me, I was taken by the Costa Rican police and placed in an orphanage in San Jose. There I stayed until an American Vietnam vet, came looking for a child to adopt.

My "now" father said he had been to several places to visit children. Yet he didn't feel the Holy Spirit saying yes to adopting them. Then he came to the orphanage where I was staying. All the other children were saying "pick me, pick me!" I on the other hand was not begging to be picked. You see, I had learned at a young age not to trust anyone and did not want to get hurt. As a matter of fact, when my father tried to pick me up, I bit him! Believe me, it probably hurt him because I had very pointed teeth and according to him, I drew blood yikes! My teeth were rotten from the sugarcane I had been living on. You would think that me biting him would detour my dad from wanting to adopt me, but it didn't. My father claims that the Holy Spirit told him, "This little girl is the one." So, my father asked the person running the orphanage, "Why does this little girl turn her back on me while the other children want to be adopted?" The woman said, "Carmen doesn't want to be rejected and we believe she has given up."

You see I was so malnourished that I couldn't even walk, and I was three years old. The doctor's told my father that if he chooses to adopt me there would be a lot of challenges to overcome. I probably wouldn't get past a D average in school. I probably would not graduate from high school, get married, or even have children. The missionary named Milre Lisso, who had been going around with my father helping him find a child, said "Oh Steve." He knew he had to take me home. I believe he called my "soon to be" mother who lived in Wichita, Kansas and told her everything he knew about me. She shared that her church and the people there prayed over me. My mom believes to this day, that I was healed that day.

So, after a thorough checkup from the doctors and all the reasons why adopting me was probably not the best choice, Steve Crane, a Vietnam vet, took me home to the United States.

With a long flight, riding with a stranger when we got off from the plane to meet the woman who would become my "mother." Dad said, "Carmen, mama" I was more than happy to jump out of his arms and into hers.

My parents told me that for the first two years due to the severe malnourishment I could not walk, but I could scoot really fast. Anytime we would have dinner I would hide some of my food. This was just in case there wouldn't be enough later. I know now that is somewhat normal for children who have been abandoned. They also said that I had a terrible fear of doctors. If I thought there was a doctor anywhere near by, I would completely fall apart and was unconsolably. These are just a few of the examples of how being abandoned can affect a child.

More Reflection:

And we know that God causes all things to
work for good to those who love God, to
those who are called according
to His purpose.

Romans 8:28 (NAS)

Knowing that I was adopted, and all the things I had been spared from, I believed myself to be a thankful child. I have to say one of the things that I really appreciate is that my father would tell me about Costa Rica and how beautiful a country it was. He said I should try to go back there and see for myself. He told me stories about the missionary who helped with my adoption and all the other things she did while on the mission field. My parents had different items from Costa Rica in the house that were made there. They also had Spanish records that I could listen to. They never wanted me to forget where I came from. Not once did I hear them say anything negative about my "biological" mother. These things were always in the back of my mind.

I believed myself to be a thankful child for all the opportunities I had been given, yet there was an underlying struggle. At age five, I remember having my first vivid dream. An angel came and showed me all these children of many colors. In the dream I was older with long brown and grey hair. I was also wearing glasses. The angel said, "someday you will be working with all these children, and you will tell them that Jesus loves them." The dream was so real, when I woke up, I wrote it down in the diary that mom had gotten for me. The handwriting and spelling were not that great for a five-year-old, but I wrote it down to remind me of what I thought was going to be my calling at the time. So, in my heart I have always had love for children of all nationalities.

My parents had a field at the back of the house, and in the field was a large rock. Sometimes, I would go there to pray or talk to God. The wind would blow in my face and through my hair. If I sat quietly and just listened, it seemed He would meet me there. Sometimes a short song would run through my mind as I enjoyed all the beautiful things God had created. This was when I first realized that I just had to sing and write these songs down that the Lord was giving me. Here is my very first song:

I love the way the wind goes round

I love how the sun goes down

Someday I won't have to frown

Because I love you Lord

I love the way the birds fly

I love the big blue sky

Someday I won't have to cry

Because I love you Lord

(Carmen Mills)

At that time, that song gave me comfort. I was struggling with sadness even back then at age five but didn't understand at the time why. Many of these things wouldn't be understood until I was an adult and had been in counseling.

Chapter 2: Worship You, The Accident

Worship the Lord with Gladness, come before him with joyful songs. Know the Lord is God. It is he who made us, and we are his people and the sheep of his pasture.

Psalms 100:2-3 (NIV)

In the summer of August 1986, I would be entering the ninth grade. I was so excited that summer! A camp that I had been going to since elementary, was getting ready to start and I was going to be a teen camper finally.

During the day, I needed to go home for band camp because I had joined Crimson Illusion. This was the flag core for John Glenn High School, we marched with the band in parades danced, and twirled flags. When practice was over, my parents would drive me back to Elkhart, so I could attend the afternoon evening part of teen/family camp.

One afternoon, my grandmother, who was one of the sweetest ladies I ever knew, was going to drive me back to camp. My parents had other obligations that day. At the time, they had adopted three more children so there were six of us all together. They definitely had a lot going on. So, grandma drove me back to camp in a brand-new little car my parents had just bought. Teen camp was having a talent show that night, so my mind was preoccupied with the song I was going to sing. Did I know the lyrics, or would I be so nervous that I would forget the words and music? Did my hair look okay, and had I chosen the right outfit? After all, I was a highschooler now. Then my grandmother said, "Carmen we should put our seatbelts on." I said, "Okay." I don't remember anything after that. When I woke up there was an EMT leaning over me, he told me not to move. I turned my head slightly and saw my grandmother not moving on the driver's side. She said, "I'm sorry." The EMT came back and told me we had been in an accident and that help was on way to get us out of the car. They put a tube by my mouth to suck up the blood that I was swallowing from the cut in my mouth. Apparently, I had bitten much of my tongue off and it was just hanging there bleeding. I vaguely remember the ride to the hospital in the ambulance. I think I was in so much pain that I just shut down for a while. In the hospital, I sort of remember seeing my parents there. But mostly remember the shot they put in my mouth so they could numb it, to sew it with stitches. Don't remember much after that. Just glad that mom and dad were there.

The next morning, I remember thinking, *Well, that was a bad dream.* Turned my head to look at my alarm clock and was thinking, *Oh, no I'm late for band camp! I'm goanna get in trouble.* When I tried to pick my head up it was sore. My head felt fat, and my mouth was swollen too. Then I realized my room smelt like flowers. So, I tried to call out to mom and realized I could not talk. This wasn't a dream; I really had been hurt. At some point mom came in and explained to me that my grandma and I had been in a car accident. I had hit my head really hard on the dashboard and when it went back to the head rest my jaw had clamped down and I had bitten most of my tong off. Thankfully, the doctor was able to sew it back together. Part of the engine from the car had smashed my kneecap. To this day I still have trouble with it, but thankful to be alive. So, for a teenager who believes she has been called to sing and write music, biting your tongue off is not good news. The doctor told me it would heal eventually but I would struggle with controlling it. Like for instance, he said, "You will probably bite it a lot." Which I do. And we weren't too sure if singing was going to be an option for me anymore. When the people at Prairie Camp heard about my accident, they lifted me and my grandmother up in prayer. Before camp was completely over my parents took me out there to sit at the camp site. They thought maybe that would cheer me up. At the time, I could only drink chicken broth and water. The teens were so kind, they came over and visited me for a little bit. That gave me so much encouragement that I didn't want to just sit at the campsite. I wanted to be with my friends. That goes to show you the power of Godly friendships. This was more evidence of God's healing power. Since that summer and the accident, I have gone on to write/record and sing music. God is so good!

Chapter 3: Protect Them Lord

Be anxious for nothing, but in everything by
prayer and supplication with thanksgiving
let your requests be made known to God

Philippians 4:6 (NIV)

When I was in the orphanage, I shared a crib with a little girl. I had always promised myself that if I ever had a daughter her name would be Melana, in honor of my crib mate.

So here I am five years later, after the doctors said I would probably never get married, or have children, now married to a wonderful Christian man. I had just had my first baby and she was a girl. So, just like I had always said I would, we named her Melana Jeanette Mills. I was so in awe at how little a person she was. She had a tiny nose, and lots of black hair at that time. Now it's brown and curly. Her face was beautiful and resembled many of her father's traits. As I would watch Melana sleep, all I ever wanted was to protect this trusting baby, who didn't seem to have a care in the world. This was very different than what I went through as a toddler: untrusting and hungry. I prayed God would watch over her night after night. She looked so safe and secure, and this was something I never wanted to see change. From all the abandonment issues that I had struggled with. Studies say that the first three years of a baby's life are the formulative ones. It's important to make sure they are loved, held, and fed. Those are the things that children in orphanages don't have due to poverty. That was not going to be the case for my little girl.

Later though, after having four daughters, I found out, you can't protect them from everything. There are lessons they must learn on their own. It seemed that the more I wanted to love my girls, something inside would become more insecure. It felt as if I was never "good" enough or "did" enough to be their mother. These negative thoughts seemed to be constantly in the forefront of my mind. I slowly became "afraid" of caring for my children too much. If I loved them, they would be taken away from me. I even started to wonder "why" did my biological mother really give me up? I knew what I had been told by my parents but wondered if there was more to the story. Maybe, back then, I hadn't been good enough, or worth keeping. Whatever the reason was, now I felt insecure in my own abilities to raise these children.

I was still a college student when I had Melana. I went to drop her off at the babysitters' house and to my horror, I had forgotten her baby formula! My heart sank, how could a mother forget her baby's food? This was when things started to spiral downward. Questioning everything. Wondering why God would entrust such a gift to a woman who didn't seem to keep things together.

These were the very first signs of depression and some of my issues from adoption and abandonment were starting to surface.

Where had my rock gone? The place where I could go for solitude. Why was it now so difficult to talk to my heavenly Father? He had been my best friend for so long and now I couldn't even find Him. I felt so alone.

Chapter 4: The Depression

"This is my commandment that you love one another, just as I have loved you."

John 15:12

This is a conflict in the Christian life since we are called to love our brother. So, I knew the scriptures, had heard it all my life. It was easier when I was younger, but as a new mother it seemed much harder. Which you think would be the other way around. Maybe I didn't want to hear the criticisms of others or feel put down. Especially when it came to my children; that was a touchy area. For whatever reason my heart was starting to shrink, and the anger was growing.

All the things I once enjoyed or looked forward to, didn't even seem to matter anymore. I remember thinking, what's the point of trying? I had even convinced myself that I was nothing, but a loser and I didn't deserve to have children. My mother had given me up so why did I think I could do any better? Do you know what happens to anger turned inward? I do now, it becomes depression. Yes, I said it, and I admitted it. The happy and carefree person I once knew had disappeared. I was now an angry and unhappy woman, mad at the world and I didn't even know why?

Could anyone help me? My husband tried but was unable to understand where I was coming from. How could he when I didn't understand the war inside myself? Everything around me seemed so hard and I wondered if I would ever get far with the things I was supposed to be accomplishing (or so at that time I thought I needed to be doing.)

This went on for several years and had gotten to the point where I didn't trust anyone. I hadn't even been praying or asking God for help. I just kept sinking deeper into the guilt that was now hanging over me. The guilt of not being able to keep up with the house and the responsibilities of being a mom and homemaker. That made me feel guilty because I knew there were people in other countries who literally have nothing (like me as a baby) and would love to be in my situation.

So, knowing where I originally came from, you would think I would be happy just having a house. Instead, I resented the place. It was a constant reminder of the things I was not good at! Yes, depression and the guilt of struggling with it are not a good tool for a stay-at-home mother. It robs you of all the things you could be enjoying at this stage in your life and the lives of your children.

So how does one change their situation when they don't know what the source of the problem is?

Romans 7:15, "I do not understand what I do. For what I want to do I do not do, but what I hate I do."

Does this scripture make sense to me? You better believe it. This is exactly how I felt. I wanted so badly to get up and clean my house or pay bills. I wanted to play with my daughters, but all I could seem to do was turn on the television and lay back on the couch. I was tired all the time and didn't have any energy.

My friends would call, but I didn't want to go out with them either. I was afraid they would judge my appearance or look at the inside of my car. I seemed to only find the things that I couldn't do well and that was my focus. Each passing day seemed longer and lonelier. Would this pain that I couldn't even describe ever come to an end? I knew the Bible, why couldn't I grasp the concept of scripture and its Word? How could I ever sing again when there was so much sadness inside me? Would I ever feel joy or happiness again?

Chapter 5: Can't Live a Day Without You

This is what the Lord, the God of your father David, says: 'I have heard your prayer and seen your tears; I will heal you.'

2 Kings 20:5

Why Lord, when the things that I had wanted and waited for like a husband, children, and a home. Why was I now feeling this way?

So, besides the loneliness, and lack of energy, I was starting to have dizzy spells. The dizziness was so bad that I did not feel comfortable around anyone. I was positive they would be able to see it in my face. I couldn't stand the way it felt anymore so I finally made a doctor's appointment. She wasn't sure what the problem was, so I went to the hospital for a few tests. Nothing was found so it was determined that I had vertigo. There was nothing that could be done, I just had to deal with it. There were many times I just wanted to be left alone.

I would even tell my husband that he needed to find a better wife and mother for the girls. How was I to function as a mother when I couldn't even concentrate on what my girls were saying to me? So let me live alone in my world of misery. I used to cry night after night, "Please God remove this dizziness from me, I can't go on this way!" One of the things I truly believe about God is, there's no point in not being honest about how you feel. He already knows everything you're thinking and feeling. I hadn't lost that part of my relationship with Him. But man was I struggling!

This whole thing went on for a year. Very alone and very depressed. It was like a deep pit that I couldn't pull myself out of. One night I had my face buried into the sofa, I was crying "again." Pleading with the Lord, these words came into my head. "Tired and broken, fragile as can be. Wishing sometimes, it just wasn't me. But you have a purpose for what I'm going through. Right now, God, it's hard trusting you. You say you love me and that you care. Please don't let me fall into despair. Don't let me live another day alone. Don't let me have another hour of my own? Don't let me get too far from your sight, and in your power and might, I'm crying to you. "Who would have thought years later that I would be singing those very words in front of other people, encouraging them not to give up. That there is hope in God and his son Jesus Christ."

At that point, I stopped asking God to remove the dizziness, but to just draw near to me. I decided to complain no longer about my situation and chose to be thankful that He loved me.

Chapter 6: If Jesus Is for Me

He heals the broken hearted and
binds up their wounds.

Psalms 149:9, NIV

I accepted the fact that for now I had vertigo. There had to be a reason for this trial and God had a plan. I tried very hard not to talk about the vertigo or clue the family in that it sometimes still bothered me. On occasion my husband would ask if I was doing all right? "For the most part" would be my typical answer. Of course, Robb wanted me to be honest with how I felt. I was determined not to complain, and grumbling was now out of the question. The enemy was not going to defeat me. "For greater is he that is in me than he that is in the world."

In August of 2006, our family was attending Prairie Camp in Elkhart. We had been going to this camp for the last nine years. Our girls really looked forward to camp. This was the same camp I went to growing up. As I had shared earlier, I had been in a bad car accident one summer heading there. For my husband and I, it was a time of renewal with the Lord. I can't really say it was restful since both of us worked in the nursery. As a family, we loved camp.

A dear sister and friend at camp noticed that I didn't feel well. She asked me about it, but I really didn't want to discuss it. Up to that point I had done a pretty good job pushing my friendships away. Not a fault of theirs, but mine. I was still struggling with depression, sickness etc. At least I was praying more and seeking a better relationship with God, so that helped.

The girls were having a good time with all the activities at camp. Robb seemed to be enjoying the evening services and so was I. However, I did not go to the alter when it was open. I felt I was handling my problems and the people from camp didn't need to know about it.

During the day, we were able to have wonderful fellowship with other nursery workers. While holding the babies we could talk and pray. There was a man named Carlos in the nursery. He suggested that I keep writing songs and not give into the vertigo. So far, I had only written one song in quite a while. It was difficult to focus, so to me, that was a tall order. I felt so lazy, it had been such a long few months.

Another camper had heard that there was a pastor who was praying with people after evening service. You could pray for anything, even healing. *This is very interesting,* I thought. I didn't want to get my hopes up and then be disappointed with God. I felt I had come so far with all of this. I still had so much to learn. Thursday night, as camp was starting to end. I still hadn't gone to the alter, nor had I gone to see this pastor that I had heard about, I was dragging my feet. Robb asked me, "Would you like to pray with the pastor?" "I don't know, he looks pretty busy." That's when Pastor Jim looked over and asked if he could help us. Robb started to explain "My wife Carmen has some health issues. We thought maybe you would pray with us?"

Jim said, "absolutely, Carmen, tell me about what's been going on this past year." So, I'm sharing everything that's been happening. The vertigo, depression, struggling with being a homemaker and wife. And losing the desire to sing or write songs. He told me "It's no accident that this has happened to you. You are working for the kingdom of God and the enemy doesn't like it. You have caught his attention. He is working hard to divert you from your calling. We need to pray and ask God for his protection. To remove this from you."

The camp tabernacle has a prayer room off to the side. That's where we went to pray. Pastor Jim's wife joined us there. Another young lady who just came by to say "hi" decided to join in too. So, there we were in the prayer room and pastor Jim started to pray for healing. He asked me to think back to my earliest memories as a child. I remember laying on a table and people were hurting me. The doctors were sticking needles in my arms, and it hurts! My stomach hurts too, I'm so hungry! I'm alone and afraid. Where are my parents and where is my mother? Doesn't anyone care that these people are hurting me? Jim said, "Carmen, you are not alone. God is with you. You need to forgive your parents." I don't know why, but when he told me, that my back began to hurt. I said, "I can't, I cannot forgive people I don't even know!" Again, he said, "Carmen, you must forgive them so that you can be free." The more he said that the more the pain in my back grew. By now I was crying. Jim then asked me, "Why are you crying?" "I don't know, just that my back is in a lot of pain."

He prayed, "Satan you have no power here, spirit of unforgiveness, you are to leave her alone! In the name of Jesus!"

At that moment something pulled up the side of my back and up into my neck. I cried some more, from the pain and then my husband started to pray too. Jim said, "In the name of Jesus, leave now!" The pain left as quickly as it had come. Something felt different, my mind felt clear, though I was kind of tired. It felt like I lost a good ten pounds. All I wanted was to smile, for the first time in quite a while I had real joy!

Chapter 7: Won't You Heal Me Now

Seek the Lord and his strength; seek his presence continually!

Psalms 105:4

So, I had been able to let go of some of the hurt I had felt being given up as a baby. This can be a hard thing to talk about with other people. They don't understand why you can't just get over it and be thankful. I believe, we as adopted children, are thankful but there will still be that struggle. I know there will always be some unanswered questions that will never be resolved.

There was a lady who was looking for someone to babysit her niece and nephew. I was a stay-at-home mom raising my four girls and I was still dealing with the vertigo. I could tell she really needed the help, so I figured I'd give it a try.

She brought the two children over and explained the situation and why she needed a babysitter. It touched my heart to hear of her willingness to raise these kids.

You could tell the older sibling was very protective of her little brother. She was only five years old herself. She pretended to have long hair. She had very short brown hair and told me that it used to be long. Then she said, "I know my mommy love's me, but I know she's not happy. Maybe I will get to go back home?" I wanted so badly to reach out and hug her and tell her that she might be able to see her mom again. Instead, I felt cold and numb. Surely, I could muster up some kind of feeling for this girl. It seemed to bring back a reminder of the rejection I felt. I had forgiven my parents, yet here it was again! There was so much expression and concern in this little girl's face. I wanted to reach out to her and her brother. Yet something held me back. At that point it no longer mattered what my struggles were, I needed to show her compassion.

I prayed right there on my sofa. "Lord, please heal me now, change my broken heart. Despite the rejection that I have felt. Help me to reach out to her and her brother. Give me the strength to be kind, to reject the wounds from my mind. Let me be a person who can show her a light in a time when her world seems so dim. She needs a mother's love, help me to love again."

I wanted so badly to be healed from this thing that plagued me with sadness, I wanted to be a good babysitter. I wanted to be a good mother too. I just kept praying and seeking the Lord for comfort. Looking back on this, I now realize that I had severe depression. At that time, I didn't know what depression was. It wasn't something that you would talk about. I mean Christians were supposed to be happy, joyful, grateful. If I truly loved God (which I did) I wouldn't feel this way. I used to be so ashamed of myself for feeling sad and trying to hide the sadness just kept me more isolated from others, it just didn't make sense. I'm happy to say that eventually the vertigo subsided. I still seek the Lord for comfort and strength. He is my rock my salvation.

Chapter 8: I Look To You

And those who know your name put their trust in you, for you, O Lord, have not forsaken those who seek you.

Psalms 9:10

Not too long ago after opening for another band in Illinois, a sweet young lady came up to me and said she really appreciated my honesty of struggling with depression and anxiety. She wanted to know, "When does the healing start?" or better yet, "When did you get your healing?" I had to sit there and think really hard, "When did my healing begin?" Had I truly been healed? I believe that I received physical healing the day that pastor from Prairie Camp prayed with me several years ago. There was another sickness that I hadn't quite overcome. The only thing was I wasn't even aware there was a problem, and it didn't come to light until my girls were much older.

Like I stated earlier, when the girls were babies, I worried that I wouldn't be a good mother. The fear of abandonment was so deep seeded, I believe I hung on to these girls tightly hoping they would never want to leave. Well, we both know realistically that it doesn't work out like that. Eventually, your children will start to spread their wings and want to do more on their own. It started with my oldest daughter. Ugh, she met a boy. Now mind you, she had talked to boys before, but this was different. I could sense her pulling away. He wasn't a bad guy or anything, but it felt as if he was stealing my daughter, my baby! I finally decided to get counseling to figure out why her dating him seemed so painful.

After weeks of talking to this Christian counselor, it came to light that I had abandonment issues. This stemmed from losing my mother during my toddler years. It wasn't that my daughter or her boyfriend did anything wrong.

It's just I saw her through my lenses (as the doctor put it).

We were able to work through this and now she is married to this wonderful man. They have a handsome son. Keep in mind I have four daughters, so I had to go through them dating three more times. It never really gets easy watching your children grow and leave home, but it's part of the process. Something you must go through when you choose to have children. The truth be told, you want them to move out as healthy, happy, humans. So, if you did your job right. (Not perfect by any stretch) there is reward when they come back.

I will admit that I did take medication during the girls dating years. Looking back on things, I probably could have used it when they were younger. It can be tricky trying to figure out which med is the right one. So, I had to go through several. I continued counseling combined with meds and exercise. Prayer is also a huge part of overcoming any type of struggle. I can't imagine getting through life without it. Still wondering when the healing took place. I believe for me it's an ongoing process. Since stepping into my calling of singing/writing and recording, I choose to go off from medication all together. I'm not saying that you should feel guilty if you need it. I just didn't want some of the side effects anymore. As an artist, I feel I need to be able to feel things so I can be authentic when singing and sharing my testimonies. There are days I still struggle but at least I'm aware of why I struggle.

Standing in from left to right: Carmen, Michaela (daughter) holding grandson,Melana (daughter),Merissa (daughter) Kneeling Miranda (daughter). Standing in the front, the other two grandsons.

Chapter 9: There Will Come a Time

Now, in all these things we are more than conquerors through him who loved us.

Romans 8:37, ESV

This time in my life things were changing rapidly. Three of my girls had moved out. Two married and one in college. It is amazing how quickly the time passed. Now, we were down to one child living at home and she was already in high school. All the years of struggling with depression and being a good enough mom seemed like such a waste. Now I was entering that realization of being an empty nester. I knew my girls were going to be all right. They all had such great gifts and potential. Now the thought of not being a full-time mother made me more even more anxious. It got so bad that I didn't even want to get out of bed, all I wanted to do was sleep. There was a program on every morning with a woman preacher. At first, I wasn't really listening, I liked the background noise. It seemed to quiet my thoughts. I think my husband realized that I had the same program on each morning, so he started putting the channel on every morning. I think he was hoping it would help or give me encouragement.

Well, I specifically remember one morning this lady saying. "I don't care if the only thing you do is get out of that bed, you can consider that a victory." I mumbled back, "I'm trying to." My body ached and I was so drained that it all was just too much work. I finally revealed to a friend of mine that I didn't think I could go on. She told my husband, and we had a meeting about where I was headed. To make a long story short, when all was said and done, I had been admitted to a depression unit. I cried so hard as was absolutely terrified at the thought of going there. But I knew it was something that needed to happen. I needed help. I wanted to get better and nothing else seemed to help.

There I was after a day or two of solid sleeping. That's how wiped out I was from being depressed. I remember looking out the window thinking, "How on earth did it get this bad that you ended up here?" I had signed with a Christian music promoter to have a song of mine played on Christian radio, not to long before this. Who would want to hear my songs if they knew I had been admitted here. I felt had no right to tell people about this God I believed in. What kind of testimony is this, you're just a joke and pathetic on top of it. What's going to happen if your premotor finds out? They might drop you all together. Being in the depression unit was not a great add for a Christian bumper sticker. Come follow Jesus so you can end up here, like her. The whole process was exhausting, and I just wanted to go back to my little room and sleep. To top that off I wasn't convinced that I even wanted to wake up! Still, I knew even in this dark moment with my mind behaving so badly, Jesus was still there.

After days of therapy, taking classes with others who were admitted there, and being put on new medication. There was the difficult task of meeting with a psychologist and sharing my past with them. When the sessions were over, and I had been there awhile I started to feel better. I even had a desire to live again (that was huge).

It had been determined that I suffered with clinical bipolar depression combined with anxiety. In some ways

I was relieved to finally have answers for my behavior and the constant years of sadness. Yet, it also scared me to think that I had a "mental illness." It took me a long time to accept that this wasn't going to just go away. I do appreciate the analogy that was used to describe taking medication. If you have a thyroid condition, you take Synthroid, thyroid meds. If you have high or low blood pressure, you take meds for that too. Clinical depression isn't that different, it's something that can be treated. I was also told that some of my depression stemmed from being abandoned. Yet, some of it could be hereditary.

When it was determined that I was getting better and could leave in a few days I was excited yet a little scared. I was happy at the thought of being home with my husband and daughter. Yet scared at not having the protection of the hospital staff to look after me. The new meds made me very tired, so I slept quite a bit, but each day got slightly better. The enemy did not win this fight and I would be singing the praises of the Lord yet again.

Chapter 10: Into the Light of Jesus

*"Because the sovereign Lord helps me, I will
not be disgraced. Therefore, have I set my
face like flint, and I know I will
not be put to shame."*

Isaiah 50:7

When I write and sing, I try to be as transparent about who I am as an artist, wife, mother, homemaker, singer/ songwriter. My life has changed, I'm not the same, I'm free from shame. Sharing this journey of being adopted and someone who has a mental illness is not easy. It has, in fact, caused me to lose some friendships. The topic makes some people uncomfortable. For others, it's the belief that if you have enough faith, it won't be an issue. In the darkest times you will find out who your friends truly are. That's when looking to people can be a huge disappointment. My counselor once said, "If you have one great friend in this life, consider yourself lucky." I've had to rely on God. People are flawed and it's okay. God is not, He is perfect. I truly believe there are many other Christians who have the same issues. Yet like me, they are ashamed and embarrassed to admit they need help. It's my heart's desire for others to understand, you are not alone. Depression is real, it's ok to ask for help. I've been asked, if this God that you believe in loves you as much as you say, then why are you plagued with this. To that I'm not sure. We live in a fallen world. In this world you will have troubles but take heart; "I have overcome the world." (John 16:33) ESV

I guess for me it's a strong faith, **Hebrews 11:1 Faith is the substance of things hoped for the evidence of things not seen.** This is one of my favorite scriptures. When I sense sadness starting to come over me, I repeat that scripture in my head. I try to see each day as a gift, that I get to get out of bed and start again. Instead of, "Oh no, it's Monday." I say things like, "What can I accomplish today?" I find making lists helps me too. There's something about crossing off a task I've completed. It does not have to be big, just that I woke up that morning and made it. These are little things I use to combat depression.

Someday there will come a time when every tear, sadness, pain, loneliness will be wiped away. I also find that singing worship songs can put things into perspective too. There's something about lifting your voice to God that brings peace.

Chapter 11: Gratitude

I give thanks to my God always for you because of the grace of God that was given you in Christ Jesus.

1 Corinthians 1:4

So, I have had parents who have adopted children or considering adoption ask me for my opinion. I am not an expert in this area. I have studied psychology in college and have a degree in Early Childhood Ed. Having said that, I am merely sharing my personal experience.

When you adopt a child, you are taking on the responsibility of the baggage that comes with them. I personally believe this is a high calling. I'm so grateful that my parents were willing to meet this challenge knowing full well I would have issues. I think about how hard my mom would try to show me she loved me, and I seemed to push back. I didn't mean to be difficult, I wanted to show her that I loved her too. Something held me back from hugging her or showing that kind of affection. I remember this song came to me after my mom was diagnosed with dementia.

> "You were a blessing, and I didn't even know it.
> You were a blessing, and I couldn't even show it.
> How could I be so blind
> When you were there all the time."
> **(Carmen Mills)**

I had been longing to meet my biological mother all this time when here this woman loved me and wanted to give me what I was searching for. It still breaks my heart that I could have done a better job showing her that I was grateful. She deserved that. My mother poured herself not only in me, but the other children they had adopted and the many children they fostered too. I truly learned a lot from this woman. My love of scripture defiantly comes from her. Not to mention the many voice lessons, organ lessons, and talent shows she took me to. Mom was a huge influence when it came to my singing. She has gone on to be with the Lord, I look forward to the day when I can say thank you, to give her a big hug without feeling awkward. At my mom's funeral, I made a promise that I would never stop singing for the Lord, I would use the gifts that He had blessed me with. The gifts that mom worked so hard to cultivate when I was younger.

I will praise the name of God with a song; I will magnify him with thanksgiving. (ESV)

If you have a child like this, give it time, they will eventually come around. I did.

So, to anyone who has adopted, fostered, or provided childcare. I pray a special blessing for you.

Mary Crane (my mother)

Steve and Mary Crane (my parents)

Robb (husband) andCarmen holding grandson.

Can You Believe It? / I Can

*Rejoice always, pray without ceasing, give
thanks in all circumstance; for this is the
will of God in Christ Jesus for you*

1 Thessalonians 5:16-18

I have shared earlier the importance of how the first three years of an infant's life are formulated and that my father was told there would be lots of complications due to lack of nutrition. These sorts of things keep following me even up to my upper years. I have been struggling with chronic pain for quite some time. Several doctors have tried to figure out what the base of the problem is but can't seem to find any answers. So, I was put into the category of fibromyalgia. This means we don't really know what's wrong with you physically, possibly mentally, but you are "broken." There's that word again, it doesn't have a good connotation but that's the label.

I recently saw a chiropractic specialist who did a complete body x-ray and heat scan. When my husband and I went for the consultation to go over the x-rays he seemed rather excited to share his findings! He said, "Quite frankly, you are an anomaly." Meaning the bones in my upper neck were fused together. He said, " I'm not trying to blame your mother or anything, but apparently you didn't have very good nutrition at the start of your life!" I then shared my story of the poverty I came out of and how my birth mom couldn't feed me. My diet consisted of sugar cane and water. I also shared about being so weak that I couldn't even walk until I was three.

The doctor said, "That sheds a lot of light for the findings of my x-rays and how the whole thing made sense now. Luckily the fusion in my neck isn't dangerous, but it is not "normal" either." He looked into my eyes and said with true compassion. "I know you are in a lot of pain, but I believe I can help you."

The Sunday before that consultation, we had been visiting a church. During the worship time they sang a song about healing and the words were, "Don't tell me God can't do it, I've seen Him heal before." I had raised my hands up and prayed, "God I don't know what's wrong with me, the doctors don't know what's wrong with me, but You do."

So, to sit in that office and go back over the beginning stages of my life as an infant, and how he felt he could help. That put more pieces of the puzzle together. I know that this process won't be easy, but I am looking forward to the result. We don't know how much time we have here on this earth. I do know; however, I don't want to waste the precious gift I have been given.